Who Is Jesus?

**DEVOTIONS
ON THE
GOSPEL OF JOHN
FOR TEENS**

Book 1

Who Is Jesus?

ABBY **VAN SOLKEMA**

REFORMED
FREE PUBLISHING
ASSOCIATION
Jenison, Michigan

© 2023 Reformed Free Publishing Association

All rights reserved

Printed in the United States of America

No part of this publication may be reproduced, stored in a retrieval system, or transmitted in any form or by any means—electronic, mechanical, photocopying, recording, or otherwise—without the prior written permission of the publisher. The only exception is brief quotations in printed reviews.

Scripture cited is take from the King James (Authorized) Version

Reformed Free Publishing
1894 Georgetown Center Drive
Jenison, MI 49428
www.rfpa.org
mail@rfpa.org

Cover design by Erika Kiel
Interior design by Katherine Lloyd / theDESKonline.com

ISBN: 978-1-944555-92-4
Ebook ISBN: 978-1-959515-05-0
LCCN: 2023946998

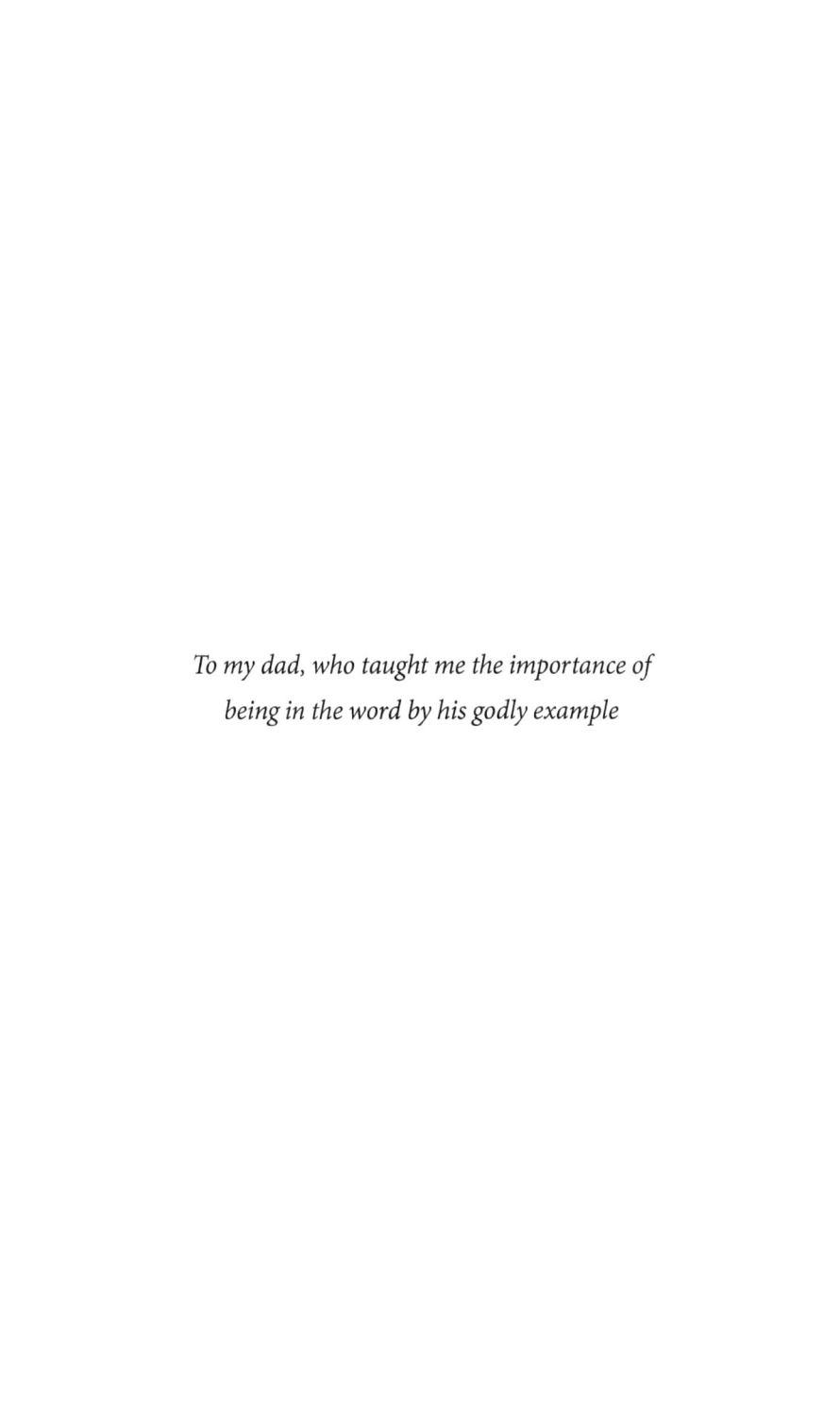

*To my dad, who taught me the importance of
being in the word by his godly example*

INTRODUCTION

Who is Jesus? This is the question that the apostle John answers in many ways with his account of Jesus' earthly ministry. John wrote the most theological of the four gospels. He included unique material that is not contained in Matthew, Mark, and Luke. Since John wrote his gospel account later, he was able to give information that helps the reader to better understand the events of the other three "synoptic," or similar gospels.

As an apostle, John was an eyewitness to Jesus' earthly ministry. He was divinely inspired to use his own witness, the testimony of John the Baptist, the Old Testament Scriptures, and Jesus' own words to write his narrative. He brought all these elements together to paint a full picture of exactly who Jesus is.

As you read through the first four chapters of John over the next twenty-eight days, I pray that you will see how important your own answer to the question, "Who is Jesus?" really is. Contrary to what many believe today, the truth of Jesus' deity, humanity, and character is not something that you can form your own opinion on. It is clearly taught in the pages of Scripture and is "profitable for doctrine, for reproof, for correction, for instruction in righteousness" (2 Tim. 3:16).

This truth has direct implications for your daily life. I pray that you will come to realize how the truth of God's word that was written so many years ago still speaks to the many issues that you face as a Christian young person today. But above all, I pray that your study of John will help you to grow in your personal relationship with your heavenly Father.

The structure of each day will be as follows: you will first read a passage from John, noting the bold-faced key phrase.

Then you will be guided to think about what the passage means by reading the meditation. The "Ask Yourself" section will assist you in applying the truth of Scripture to your life. And finally, the "Praying to Your Heavenly Father" section lists three prayer prompts based on this passage that you can use as a starting point for your own prayer. The journaling space can be used to record your thoughts on the application questions or to write out your prayer.

This volume and the three that will follow are not a comprehensive commentary on the gospel according to John. Rather, they are meant to be a guide to systematically lead you through an entire book of the Bible while familiarizing you with the process of personal Bible study. If you have any questions about the verses that you are reading, I encourage you to talk about them with your parents and siblings, discuss them with godly friends, or go to an elder or pastor for help.

JOHN 1:1-3

In the beginning was the Word, and the Word was with God, **and the Word was God.**

The same was in the beginning with God.

All things were made by him; and without him was not any thing made that was made.

DAY 1 – **JESUS IS GOD**

Mark's gospel account starts with the beginning of Jesus' earthly ministry. Luke's begins with the birth of Jesus. Matthew's goes back even further by including the genealogy of Jesus before his birth. But the opening words of John's gospel account go back to the very beginning of the story. He echoes Genesis 1:1, "In the beginning God created the heaven and the earth." Then John points us back even farther—to eternity past—to show that not only was God the Son present at creation, *he always was.*

The second person of the Trinity did not come into existence when he came to earth as a man. The Son of God has always existed in fellowship with the Father and the Holy Spirit. As *the Word*, the visible revelation of the triune God, he had an active role in the creation of the universe. Everything was created through him and for him. He also continues to uphold and sustain all things (Col. 1:13–17). From the very beginning, John makes his main point clear: Jesus is God.

The original audience of John's gospel account in the first century was Jews and Gentiles who lived in the Greco-Roman world and the surrounding areas. They had varying responses to John's bold claim that Jesus was God. Unbelieving Jews saw John's claim as blasphemy. Many unbelieving Gentiles who were used to the idea of having many gods simply added Jesus to the list. But those given true faith, whether Jew or Gentile, believed and embraced the truth of Jesus' deity.

There are also many different responses to the truth of who Jesus is today. Some deny that Jesus exists altogether. Others see him as only a good man who lived long ago or a great moral teacher. Some may even acknowledge that Jesus came from heaven but deny the authority that his teaching should have in their life. But this passage states plainly that Jesus is nothing less than God himself.

DAY 1 – JESUS IS GOD

ASK YOURSELF...

Who do you believe that Jesus is?

....
....
....
....

How will your belief about who Jesus is affect how you read and respond to his teaching in the book of John?

....
....
....
....

PRAYING TO YOUR HEAVENLY FATHER

- This passage reminds us that our Lord is not restricted by time like humans are. *Praise* Him for his eternality!
- How do you sinfully limit God in your mind by having a view of him that is lesser than Scripture's? *Confess* this sin.
- *Thank* your heavenly Father for his continual government and care of creation.

....
....
....
....
....
....
....
....
....
....

JOHN 1:4-9

In him was life; and the life was the light of men.

And **the light shineth in darkness**; and the darkness comprehended it not.

There was a man sent from God, whose name was John. The same came for a witness, to bear witness of the Light, that all men through him might believe.

He was not that Light, but was sent to bear witness of that Light.

That was the true Light, which lighteth every man that cometh into the world.

DAY 2 – **LIGHT AND DARKNESS**

The contrast between light and darkness is a picture that is used many times in the New Testament, especially by the apostle John. You of course are familiar with the idea of light and darkness, but do you fully understand what John means when he says that Jesus is light?

Throughout Scripture, the image of light is used to show righteousness, truth, and goodness. In Psalm 119:105 we see God's word compared to a lamp that sheds light on the path of obedience to God's commands. On the other hand, the image of darkness is used to show what is sinful, false, and repulsive to God. The works of darkness are described in Romans 13:13 as partying, drunkenness, immorality, lust, fighting, and envy.

Jesus is not just light; he is the Light. As the Son of God, he is the source of all light. Even when he took on a human nature and came to this dark world, he shone as a perfect example of what is true, right, and good.

Since the fall, the natural state of this world is death and darkness. All men are not only lost in the darkness, but they prefer the darkness and cannot even comprehend the light. Yet in his mercy, God uses the light of the gospel—the truth about Jesus—to draw out of darkness those whom He has elected before the world began. This light exposes sin and irresistibly draws God's children to saving faith.

Because of Jesus' work on the cross, his people can be lights too (Eph. 5:8). In 1 Peter 2:9 we read, "But ye are a chosen generation, a royal priesthood, an holy nation, a peculiar people; that ye should shew forth the praises of him who hath called you out of darkness into his marvellous light." John the Baptist devoted his entire life to reflecting the light of Jesus into the darkness of this world so that others would believe. As a Christian young person today, you are called to do the same.

DEVOTIONS ON THE GOSPEL OF JOHN FOR TEENS

ASK YOURSELF...

What are some specific ways that your life shines as light for Jesus?

....
....
....
....

How can you improve in this area?

....
....
....
....

PRAYING TO YOUR HEAVENLY FATHER

- Is there an area of your life where you are drawn to the darkness rather than the light? *Confess* this sin.
- *Ask* God to give you the grace and courage necessary to shine as a light in this dark world.
- *Thank* God for calling you out of darkness into his marvelous light.

....
....
....
....
....
....
....
....
....
....
....

JOHN 1:10-13

He was in the world, and the world was made by him, and the world knew him not.

He came unto his own, and his own received him not.

But as many as received him, to them gave he power to become the sons of God, even to them that believe on his name:

Which were born, not of blood, nor of the will of the flesh, nor of the will of man, **but of God**.

DAY 3 – **BORN OF GOD**

Jesus came into this world as the true Light—the physical appearance of God's glory. But even though his light shone on all men, his glory was not apparent to all men. The eyes of faith were necessary to recognize it. Isaiah 53:2–3 tells us that there was nothing physically remarkable about Jesus' outward appearance. To the world he looked like an ordinary, common man—a poor carpenter's son.

Jesus also did not look like the king that the Jewish people were expecting. They were looking for a powerful earthly ruler to save them from the rule of the Roman government. When Jesus came to "his own," the people who had been given the promise of his coming, as a whole they rejected him. The Jews had ignored the prophets in the Old Testament, they ignored John the Baptist, and now they ignored Jesus himself. Because of this rejection, as a nation they lost the right to be the covenant people of God.

Yet there were some that did believe, both Jews and Gentiles. Why did these people believe and not others? Because the Holy Spirit had worked regeneration, or new life, in their hearts. Belief is evidence of this spiritual rebirth. Every child of God must be born again. This spiritual birth is an act of God, not man.

Simply being a part of the nation of Israel was not enough to make someone a child of God. Simply being a part of an earthly family who profess to be Christians also does not give you the right to be a child of God. (Although God does usually save in the line of generations.) Your assurance of your salvation must come from the work of God in your own heart and life, not from your ancestry or the earthly family to which you belong.

DAY 3 – BORN OF GOD

ASK YOURSELF...

Have you ever been tempted to trust in your place in a Christian family as the basis for your salvation, maybe without even realizing it?

....
....
....
....

Why do you think it is so tempting to trust in earthly, human things for your salvation instead of the work of God?

....
....
....
....

PRAYING TO YOUR HEAVENLY FATHER

- *Praise* God for his amazing work of regeneration (new life) in your heart.
- *Confess* your inability to believe apart from the work of the Holy Spirit in your heart.
- *Thank* God for sending the true Light into the world to save you from your sin.

....
....
....
....
....
....
....
....
....

JOHN 1:14-18

And the Word was made flesh, and dwelt among us, (and we beheld his glory, the glory as of the only begotten of the Father,) full of grace and truth.

John bare witness of him, and cried, saying, This was he of whom I spake, He that cometh after me is preferred before me: for he was before me.

And of his fulness have all we received, and **grace for grace**.

For the law was given by Moses, but grace and truth came by Jesus Christ.

No man hath seen God at any time; the only begotten Son, which is in the bosom of the Father, he hath declared him.

DAY 4 – **GRACE UPON GRACE**

In the Old Testament, God used different signs and symbols to show his presence with the nation of Israel. Can you remember any of these symbols? But in the New Testament when "the Word was made flesh" (v. 14) God came to dwell with man in a way that he never had before. The Son of God came into the world as a human being.

Jesus did not just have a small part of God in him, but every single part, the fullness of the glory of God. Jesus was the embodiment of the grace and truth of God. He was the fulfillment of all the Old Testament signs and symbols. The law that was given through Moses showed the people their sin and called them to repentance, but the grace and truth given through Jesus Christ freed people from the law and enabled them to obey it.

Peter, James, and John experienced the glory of the incarnation of the Son of God first-hand at his transfiguration. They and many others also witnessed this glory throughout Jesus' earthly ministry. God's love, grace, mercy, peace, and power were on full display in the person of Jesus during his time on this earth, culminating in his resurrection and ascension.

But even though Jesus is no longer on this earth today, God still dwells with his people. Since Pentecost, God's people experience the fullness of his grace through the gift of his Spirit in our hearts. He has also ordained means of grace by which to give blessings from heaven to those on earth.

These means of grace are the preaching of the gospel and two sacraments—holy baptism and the Lord's supper. When you hear the preaching of the gospel and partake of these sacraments by faith, you experience "grace for grace" (v. 16), meaning grace upon grace upon grace, all heaped up on each other. Do you realize what an amazing blessing this is?

ASK YOURSELF...

Are you a confessing member of a church where the truth of the gospel is preached?

....
....
....
....

Are you able to fully participate in the Lord's supper? If not, prayerfully consider if God is leading you to make public confession of your faith so that you may take part in these means of grace.

....
....
....
....

PRAYING TO YOUR HEAVENLY FATHER

- *Confess* a time when you have taken the means of grace for granted.
- *Ask* for guidance as you consider your own church membership.
- *Thank* God for the abundance of grace that he showers on you though the Holy Spirit.

....
....
....
....
....
....
....
....

JOHN 1:19-23

And this is the record of John, when the Jews sent priests and Levites from Jerusalem to ask him, Who art thou?

And he confessed, and denied not; but confessed, I am not the Christ.

And they asked him, What then? Art thou Elias? And he saith, I am not. Art thou that prophet? And he answered, No.

Then said they unto him, Who art thou? that we may give an answer to them that sent us. What sayest thou of thyself?

He said, **I am the voice of one crying in the wilderness,** Make straight the way of the Lord, as said the prophet Esaias.

DAY 5 – **A WAY IN THE WILDERNESS**

Prior to the ministry of John the Baptist, God had been silent for about four hundred years. In the time between the Old and New Testaments there were no new prophets. Ever since Malachi, there had been no word from God.

Many of the people probably thought God had forgotten about them. The Romans ruled over Israel and there was no king from the line of David on the throne. The spiritual landscape of the church was that of a barren desert, dry and hopeless.

It was onto this bleak scene that John the Baptist emerged. He called the people to repent from their sins and be baptized to prepare their hearts to receive their Savior. He was called to make a way in this spiritual wilderness for the coming of the Messiah.

Since it had been so long since God had sent a prophet, John the Baptist's radical ministry naturally caught the attention of the Jewish leaders. They sent a delegation of priests and Levites to ask him, "Who art thou?" John made clear to them in his answer that he was not the promised Christ for whom they were waiting.

Then they wondered if he was Elias (Elijah), recalling the prophecy of Malachi 4:5. John answered, "I am not." Then they asked if he was "that prophet" (Moses), recalling the promise of Deuteronomy 18:18. John answered again, "No."

To answer their question, John turned to yet another Old Testament prophet, Isaiah. His quotation in verse 23 from Isaiah 40:3 declared to the people that he was simply a messenger from God, sent to prepare the way for the long-awaited Messiah. Although he had been silent for so many years, God had not forsaken his people. He was using all these events to prepare for his Son to come to save his people from their sins.

DAY 5 – A WAY IN THE WILDERNESS

ASK YOURSELF...

How do you see God working in the world around you to prepare for Jesus' second coming?

....
....
....
....

How are you called to prepare for the second coming? How can you improve in this area?

....
....
....
....

PRAYING TO YOUR HEAVENLY FATHER

- *Praise* God for his gracious work in the spiritual wilderness of your heart.
- *Ask* for grace to live your life in the awareness that Jesus is coming again soon.
- Give *thanks* for the continual work of Christ on your behalf as Prophet, Priest, and King in heaven.

....
....
....
....
....
....
....
....
....
....

JOHN 1:24-28

And they that were sent were of the Pharisees.

And they asked him, and said unto him, Why baptizest thou then, if thou be not that Christ, nor Elias, neither that prophet?

John answered them, saying, I baptize with water: but there standeth one among you, whom ye know not;

He it is, who coming after me is preferred before me, whose shoe's latchet I am not worthy to unloose.

These things were done in Bethabara beyond Jordan, where John was baptizing.

DAY 6 – **PREFERRED BEFORE ME**

John the Baptist's presence as a prophet after so many years of silence was not the only thing that caught the attention of the Jewish leaders. The message that he preached was radical. When John told the Jews they needed to repent and be baptized, he was asking them to do something that was particularly humbling for a Jew. Baptism was a ritual that was usually reserved for Gentile proselytes who had converted to Judaism. By telling them to be baptized, he was essentially calling them unclean. This outraged the Jewish rulers!

These Jews did not recognize that the promised Christ was living among them. They were also blinded to the fact that humility is a crucial part of the Christian life. Their focus was solely on themselves and achieving their own righteousness.

But humility was a virtue that John the Baptist understood well. The entire purpose of his ministry as a prophet was to draw attention to Christ, not himself. John had a high calling from God. Yet he humbly recognized how insignificant he was compared to the greatness of the incarnate Son of God. In his response to the delegation from the Pharisees, he stated that he was not even worthy to unlatch the shoe of Jesus. This was a task that a slave would normally do.

Humility is still a necessary part of the Christian life today. You can learn from the humility of John the Baptist. As you read on in the book of John, you will also see the perfect example of humility in Jesus during his time on this earth.

In order to be humble, Christians must have an accurate picture of self, viewed through the lens of God's word. They must see their own unworthiness by nature, but also who they are in Christ because of God's grace. A life of humility is not characterized by self-loathing, but by thankfully obeying what God has called you to do with joy and contentment. Humility is continually seeking to bring glory to his name instead of your own.

ASK YOURSELF...

Would others describe you as a humble person? Why or why not?

What are some ways that you could grow in humility?

PRAYING TO YOUR HEAVENLY FATHER

- *Praise* God for his incomprehensible greatness.
- *Confess* a time when you fell into the sin of pride.
- *Ask* God to help you grow in humility.

JOHN 1:29-34

The next day John seeth Jesus coming unto him, and saith, **Behold the Lamb of God**, which taketh away the sin of the world.

This is he of whom I said, After me cometh a man which is preferred before me: for he was before me.

And I knew him not: but that he should be made manifest to Israel, therefore am I come baptizing with water.

And John bare record, saying, I saw the Spirit descending from heaven like a dove, and it abode upon him.

And I knew him not: but he that sent me to baptize with water, the same said unto me, Upon whom thou shalt see the Spirit descending, and remaining on him, the same is he which baptizeth with the Holy Ghost.

And I saw, and bare record that this is the Son of God.

DAY 7 – **BEHOLD THE LAMB OF GOD**

John the Baptist knew that Jesus was the Son of God. About forty days before this, he himself had baptized Jesus. He saw the Spirit descend on Jesus in the form of a dove with his own eyes (Matt. 3:16). He heard firsthand the voice from heaven saying, "This is my beloved Son, in whom I am well pleased" (Matt. 3:17).

As the priests and Levites were questioning John about who he was, John carried out the purpose of his ministry faithfully. He redirected their attention to Jesus by proclaiming, "Behold the Lamb of God!" (v. 29). The figure of a lamb was one that would have been familiar to the Jewish people. God had designated lambs to be used for several burnt offerings in the Old Testament laws. The lamb as an offering also had a special place in the Passover feast as one whose blood spared that home from the angel of death.

Jesus is the Lamb of God, sent to be the ultimate sacrifice, the fulfillment of all the lambs that had died before him. We read in Isaiah's messianic prophecy that he will be "brought as a lamb to the slaughter" and that God laid on him "the iniquity of us all" (53:6–7). As one who was both fully man and fully God, the blood of the Lamb was the only sacrifice that was fit to pay the price for the sins of his people.

This proclamation of John the Baptist also comes to you today, "Behold the Lamb of God!" The word "behold" is a command to look at something. It is a command to look to Jesus as the only way of salvation. He is the only one who could take your sin upon himself and give you his perfect righteousness through the shedding of his own blood (2 Cor. 5:21).

We often struggle to keep our eyes on Jesus in this life. But because of him, we have the Spirit in our hearts to help us in this struggle. And you can look forward to the day when you will be able to spend all of eternity worshiping the Lamb of God perfectly!

ASK YOURSELF...

How do you behold the Lamb of God?

....
....
....
....

What are some things in your life that take your attention away from your Savior? How can you limit these things?

....
....
....
....

PRAYING TO YOUR HEAVENLY FATHER

- *Confess* a time when you were tempted to look to something or someone other than Jesus for your salvation.
- *Ask* for strength to fix your eyes on your Savior instead of the things of this world.
- *Thank* God for sending his own Son to be the perfect sacrifice for your sin.

JOHN 1:35–42

Again the next day after John stood, and two of his disciples; And looking upon Jesus as he walked, he saith, Behold the Lamb of God!

And the two disciples **heard him speak, and they followed Jesus.**

Then Jesus turned, and saw them following, and saith unto them, What seek ye? They said unto him, Rabbi, (which is to say, being interpreted, Master,) where dwellest thou?

He saith unto them, Come and see. They came and saw where he dwelt, and abode with him that day: for it was about the tenth hour.

One of the two which heard John speak, and followed him, was Andrew, Simon Peter's brother.

He first findeth his own brother Simon, and saith unto him, We have found the Messias, which is, being interpreted, the Christ.

And he brought him to Jesus. And when Jesus beheld him, he said, Thou art Simon the son of Jona: thou shalt be called Cephas, which is by interpretation, A stone.

DAY 8 – **CALLED TO FOLLOW JESUS**

John was divinely inspired to include more specifics regarding the gathering of Jesus' first disciples about which the other gospels do not go into detail. We can learn from these details about the means that God uses to call his people. Here we read about the calling of Andrew, Peter, and another disciple, who was most likely John himself. (The fact that he does not mention the name of the other disciple combined with the fact that he gives the specific time of day when this happened seems to indicate that the other disciple was John.)

John and Andrew both received the call to follow Jesus by means of the preaching of John the Baptist. When they began to follow Jesus, he asked them, "What seek ye?" It is clear from their answer that they were not motivated by idle curiosity at John's words, but by a true desire to learn from Jesus and live as he lived. Although John was the instrument of their calling, God worked true faith in their hearts to believe.

Andrew then went on to share his faith with his brother Simon Peter. He told Simon that they had found the "Messias" (v. 41)—the anointed one. Andrew brought Simon to Jesus, who prophesied that Simon Peter would someday be a great leader in the church.

Faithful gospel preaching is the external means by which God calls his people to himself alongside the internal work of the Holy Spirit in their hearts. This is why the church desperately needs ministers. The proclamation of the gospel is a precious way that God uses to gather and instruct his elect, "and how shall they hear without a preacher?" (Rom. 10:14).

You may not receive the special calling to be a pastor. But God can still use you to bring the truth of the gospel to those around you. You have the duty of all believers to bring others to Christ just as Andrew did with his brother Simon Peter.

ASK YOURSELF...

Young men, have you seriously and prayerfully considered whether God is calling you to be a minister of the gospel?

....
....
....
....

Young women, how are you called to share the truth of the gospel with others in your daily life?

....
....
....
....

PRAYING TO YOUR HEAVENLY FATHER

- *Confess* a time when you held back from sharing the gospel with someone because of your own fears.
- *Ask* God to be with your pastor as he faithfully preaches the gospel each week or to bring you a faithful pastor if your church is without one.
- *Thank* God for his work of grace in calling you to saving faith.

....
....
....
....
....
....
....
....
....

JOHN 1:43-51

The day following Jesus would go forth into Galilee, and findeth Philip, and saith unto him, Follow me. Now Philip was of Bethsaida, the city of Andrew and Peter.

Philip findeth Nathanael, and saith unto him, We have found him, of whom Moses in the law, and the prophets, did write, Jesus of Nazareth, the son of Joseph.

And Nathanael said unto him, Can there any good thing come out of Nazareth? Philip saith unto him, Come and see.

Jesus saw Nathanael coming to him, and saith of him, Behold an Israelite indeed, in whom is no guile!

Nathanael saith unto him, **Whence knowest thou me?** Jesus answered and said unto him, Before that Philip called thee, when thou wast under the fig tree, I saw thee.

Nathanael answered and saith unto him, Rabbi, thou art the Son of God; thou art the King of Israel.

Jesus answered and said unto him, Because I said unto thee, I saw thee under the fig tree, believest thou? thou shalt see greater things than these.

And he saith unto him, Verily, verily, I say unto you, Hereafter ye shall see heaven open, and the angels of God ascending and descending upon the Son of man.

DAY 9 – **A PERSONAL CALLING**

The next day after Andrew, John, and Peter became Jesus' disciples, Philip and Nathanael (also known as Bartholomew) were also called to follow Jesus. Jesus sought out Philip directly and commanded him, "Follow me." Then Philip found Nathanael and witnessed to him by telling him to "come and see" the promised Messiah.

Nathanael was skeptical of Philip's testimony at first since this supposed Savior had come from the lowly town of Nazareth. But he was soon convinced that this was the Son of God. When Jesus addressed him, he made clear that he already knew Nathanael's character and that he had been "under the fig tree."

Does this phrase sound a little strange to you? It was commonly used by rabbis to mean time spent meditating on Scripture. Jesus could have been using it in this way. Or maybe Nathanael had actually been sitting under a fig tree. Either way, he was clearly amazed by the wonder of Jesus' supernatural knowledge of his actions. This formerly skeptical Jew believed and confessed that Jesus is both the "Son of God" and "King of Israel" (v. 49). Then Jesus assured him that even more amazing wonders were yet to come.

As the Son of God, Jesus is omniscient, meaning he knows all things. As the good shepherd, Jesus knows the needs of every one of his sheep. He knew everything about Nathanael—his prejudice, his sincerity, his study of and meditation on Scripture.

Your Savior knows everything about you too—your strengths and weaknesses and all the intimate details of your life. He used the unique circumstances of your life to call you to him just as he called each one of his disciples. Every child of God has his or her own amazing story of being brought to salvation. Even if you were saved in a seemingly "ordinary" way through being brought to church by your parents and hearing the preaching of the gospel from a young age, your conversion is still extraordinary!

ASK YOURSELF...

How did God's providence and irresistible grace work together to bring you into union with Christ?

How does remembering the truth that your heavenly Father knows everything about you give you comfort in your daily life?

PRAYING TO YOUR HEAVENLY FATHER

- *Praise* God for his providence and irresistible grace.
- *Ask* for help to continually remember the wonder of your salvation.
- Give *thanks* to your good shepherd who lovingly provides for all your needs.

JOHN 2:1-12

And the third day there was a marriage in Cana of Galilee; and the mother of Jesus was there:

And both Jesus was called, and his disciples, to the marriage.

And when they wanted wine, the mother of Jesus saith unto him, They have no wine.

Jesus saith unto her, Woman, what have I to do with thee? mine hour is not yet come.

His mother saith unto the servants, Whatsoever he saith unto you, do it.

And there were set there six waterpots of stone, after the manner of the purifying of the Jews, containing two or three firkins apiece.

Jesus saith unto them, Fill the waterpots with water. And they filled them up to the brim.

And he saith unto them, Draw out now, and bear unto the governor of the feast. And they bare it.

When the ruler of the feast had tasted the water that was made wine, and knew not whence it was: (but the servants which drew the water knew;) the governor of the feast called the bridegroom,

And saith unto him, Every man at the beginning doth set forth good wine; and when men have well drunk, then that which is worse: but thou hast kept the good wine until now.

This beginning of miracles did Jesus in Cana of Galilee, **and manifested forth his glory**; and his disciples believed on him.

After this he went down to Capernaum, he, and his mother, and his brethren, and his disciples: and they continued there not many days.

DAY 10 – **A SIGN OF HIS GLORY**

Jesus' wonder of turning water into wine at a wedding in Cana of Galilee was the first miracle that he performed during his earthly ministry. It is also the first of only seven miracles that John included in his gospel account, though Jesus did many more.

Interestingly, John did not give a lot of details about the wedding feast where this miracle took place. We are not told who was getting married nor what their relationship to Jesus and his mother was. This is instructive because it reminds us that we should not get too caught up in the minor details of the miracles that are recorded in Scripture. Rather our focus should be on what each miracle teaches us about the glory of Christ.

The miracles that Jesus performed during his ministry were like parables in action. Each one used earthly things to reveal something about who God is and who we are not. Wine normally takes a long time to produce. Jesus' miracle of instantly changing water into fine wine shows the amazing, transforming power of God. He can transform the hearts of even the most depraved sinners according to his will.

Wine was a symbol of joy and blessing in the Old Testament (Ps. 104:15, Prov. 3:10). In the New Testament it was a symbol of Christ's blood (1 Cor. 11:25). The hosts of this wedding could not provide enough wine for their guests. But Jesus' ability to provide more wine than they needed shows how he graciously gives salvation and blessings to his people in abundance.

Just as the preaching of the gospel either draws people to Christ or drives them away (Heb. 4:12), the amazing miracles that Jesus performed had a very different effect on the two types of people who witnessed them. For believers such as Jesus' disciples, his miracles displayed his glory and grace and served to strengthen their faith. But for unbelievers, Jesus' miracles were simply fascinating tricks and even served to harden their hearts further against him.

ASK YOURSELF...

What signs of God's glory can you see in your own life?

....
....
....
....

How does meditating on this miracle of Jesus and his work in your life strengthen your faith in him?

....
....
....
....

PRAYING TO YOUR HEAVENLY FATHER...

- *Praise* God for his transforming power.
- *Ask* for the Spirit to work in your heart to strengthen your faith in God.
- Give *thanks* for the abundant joy and blessings he has given you.

....
....
....
....
....
....
....
....
....
....

JOHN 2:13-17

And the Jews' passover was at hand, and Jesus went up to Jerusalem,

And found in the temple those that sold oxen and sheep and doves, and the changers of money sitting:

And when he had made a scourge of small cords, he drove them all out of the temple, and the sheep, and the oxen; and poured out the changers' money, and overthrew the tables;

And said unto them that sold doves, Take these things hence; make not my Father's house an house of merchandise.

And his disciples remembered that it was written, **The zeal of thine house hath eaten me up.**

DAY 11 – **HOLY AND UNHOLY ZEAL**

All Jewish males over the age of twelve were expected to attend the annual Passover celebration in Jerusalem. During this week in particular, the city of Jerusalem and the temple would have been especially crowded with visitors. Merchants and moneychangers set up shop in the outer court of the temple to sell animals and exchange coins. They knew people from outside Jerusalem would need to bring sacrifices and pay the required temple tax.

This may seem convenient, but it is important to remember that the outer court was supposed to be the area where Gentiles could come and worship. It was designated by God to be a place of reverent worship. Instead it had been turned into a chaotic, bustling marketplace. When Jesus witnessed this misuse of his Father's house, he passionately took action. He fashioned a whip from small cords and used it to drive the merchants and their goods out of the temple.

As a man, Jesus experienced a full range of emotions. Yet his emotions were not corrupted by sin like ours are. The passionate anger that drove him to action here was not sinful because it was motivated by a righteous devotion to the glory of his Father.

Jesus was zealous for the purity of his Father's house and the worship of the one true God. The holy zeal that Jesus displayed here reminded his disciples of the passion that David had for God and his worship as shown in his deep desire to build the temple. They remembered David's words from Psalm 69:9: "For the zeal of thine house hath eaten me up."

It is good to be passionate about things. Even intense emotions such as anger or jealousy and the actions that result from them can be holy, but only if they arise from a godly motivation. You can be passionate about helping others, angry at sin, and jealous for God's glory. But how often when you feel strong emotions do they instead come from your own wounded pride and love of self?

DAY 11 – HOLY AND UNHOLY ZEAL

ASK YOURSELF…

When was the last time that you felt a strong emotion like anger or jealousy?

....
....
....
....

Did your emotion come from love of God or love of yourself? Did this emotion lead you to godly or ungodly action?

....
....
....
....

PRAYING TO YOUR HEAVENLY FATHER

- *Thank* the Lord for his good gift of emotions.
- *Confess* a time when your selfish emotions caused you to sin.
- *Ask* for the Spirit's help to be jealous for God's glory instead of your own glory.

....
....
....
....
....
....
....
....
....
....

JOHN 2:18-22

Then answered the Jews and said unto him, What sign shewest thou unto us, seeing that thou doest these things?

Jesus answered and said unto them, **Destroy this temple, and in three days I will raise it up.**

Then said the Jews, Forty and six years was this temple in building, and wilt thou rear it up in three days?

But he spake of the temple of his body.

When therefore he was risen from the dead, his disciples remembered that he had said this unto them; and they believed the scripture, and the word which Jesus had said.

DAY 12 – **BENEFITS OF CHRIST'S RESURRECTION**

The Jewish leaders should have been ashamed after Jesus drove the merchants and moneychangers out of the temple. They should have repented of their sin of allowing for the desecration of God's house. But instead, they sinfully questioned Jesus and demanded he give them a sign to show what authority he had to do such a thing.

Jesus' answer most likely confused everyone there. "Destroy this temple, and in three days I will raise it up" (v. 19). Everyone knew Herod had been restoring the temple for the past forty-six years. How could this man claim to raise it up in three days?

The Jews had forgotten that this beautiful earthly temple was only a shadow of the reality to which it pointed—Christ himself. He came to replace the temple and fulfill its purpose as a meeting place between God and man.

Even the disciples did not understand what Jesus was talking about, though John adds that they remembered these words after Jesus' resurrection and believed. As you look back with the knowledge of all of Scripture today, you can see the truth even more clearly. Jesus' resurrection after three days is another infallible proof that he is God.

Do you understand the importance of Christ's resurrection? Do you know what it means to "serve a risen Savior" as the Easter hymn puts it? The Heidelberg Catechism highlights three major benefits of the resurrection for you. First, the resurrection assures you that Christ purchased righteousness for you on the cross (Rom. 4:25, 1 Cor. 15:17). Second, because Christ arose, you are both called and equipped to live a new, godly life in Christ (Rom. 6:4, Col. 3:1). And finally, Christ's resurrection is a promise that your body will someday be resurrected as well (Rom. 8:11, 1 Thess. 4:13–18). Because he lives, you will live forever in heaven!

ASK YOURSELF...

Have you ever lost a loved one? How does remembering the truth of Christ's resurrection change the way that you think about their death?

....
....
....
....

How does it change the way you think about your own death?

....
....
....
....

PRAYING TO YOUR HEAVENLY FATHER

- *Praise* the Lord for his great grace in sending his only begotten Son to die and raising him from the dead.
- *Ask* for strength to "walk in newness of life" (Rom. 6:4) and "seek those things which are above" (Col. 3:1).
- *Thank* God for the great comfort that the truth of Christ's resurrection gives you.

....
....
....
....
....
....
....
....
....
....

JOHN 2:23–25

Now when he was in Jerusalem at the passover, in the feast day, many believed in his name, when they saw the miracles which he did.

But Jesus did not commit himself unto them, because he knew all men,

And needed not that any should testify of man: for **he knew what was in man**.

DAY 13 – **GOD KNOWS YOUR HEART**

The amazing miracles that Jesus did in Jerusalem during the week of Passover attracted the attention of many people. From all outward appearances, Jesus had a multitude of genuine followers. Most of these people did believe that he was a man with great power from God. But they did not believe that he was actually the Son of God. Yet Jesus was not deceived by the attention of these crowds of people because he knew "what was in man" (v. 25).

John repeated the same Greek word in these verses to drive home the point that though these crowds of people "believed" (v. 23) in Jesus, Jesus did not "commit" (v. 24) or believe in them because he knew they did not truly believe. He did not engage with these crowds of people or take the time to form a relationship with them because he knew that their interest in him was only superficial. He knew that their hearts were not changed. This knowledge is another proof of Jesus' deity because only God could know this. We call this attribute of God his omniscience, meaning his perfect knowledge of all things.

When you read about the conversion of Nathanael in John 1, you understood that God's omniscience means he knows everything about you. This passage shows that he even knows the true state of your heart. God knows if your outward worship is insincere. The deepest secrets of your heart from your past, present, and future are never hidden from him. He even knows the sins that you might lie about to yourself and keep hidden from everyone else.

The fact that your heart is known completely by your heavenly Father should remind you that it is never possible to get away with sin even if other people do not know about it. You must confess and repent of all your sins. Yet the one who knows the hearts of all men also sees that the hearts of his people have been regenerated by the Holy Spirit. He is gracious to forgive every one of your sins because of Christ's sacrifice for you on the cross.

DAY 13 – GOD KNOWS YOUR HEART

ASK YOURSELF...

Have you ever felt like you were getting away with sin because you kept it hidden from others?

....
....
....
....

When you think about how God knows your heart, how does it change the way you view your sin?

....
....
....
....

PRAYING TO YOUR HEAVENLY FATHER

- *Praise* the Lord who knows all things.
- *Confess* a sin that you try to keep hidden.
- *Ask* God to hear this prayer from Psalm 139:23–24: "Search me, O God, and know my heart: try me, and know my thoughts: and see if there be any wicked way in me, and lead me in the way everlasting."

JOHN 3:1-6

There was a man of the Pharisees, named Nicodemus, a ruler of the Jews:

The same came to Jesus by night, and said unto him, Rabbi, we know that thou art a teacher come from God: for no man can do these miracles that thou doest, except God be with him.

Jesus answered and said unto him, Verily, verily, I say unto thee, **Except a man be born again, he cannot see the kingdom of God.**

Nicodemus saith unto him, How can a man be born when he is old? can he enter the second time into his mother's womb, and be born?

Jesus answered, Verily, verily, I say unto thee, Except a man be born of water and of the Spirit, he cannot enter into the kingdom of God.

That which is born of the flesh is flesh; and that which is born of the Spirit is spirit.

DAY 14 – **TRANSFORMED INTO TRUE CITIZENS**

John 3 introduces us to a man named Nicodemus. We learn that he was a Pharisee and an influential leader of the Jews. He was also a member of the Sanhedrin (the Jewish ruling council) and a model Jew. He knew the Old Testament Scriptures well as a result of his Pharisaic training and had instructed the Jewish people in these Scriptures (3:10).

Nicodemus and all of the Jewish leaders had been keeping an eye on Jesus in Jerusalem as he performed amazing miracles. It was evident that Jesus had God-given power, but was he a prophet or something more? Nicodemus decided to come to Jesus at night to find out more about who this man was.

He greeted Jesus as "Rabbi" or teacher, which was a sign of respect since Nicodemus was older and far more educated than Jesus was from an earthly perspective. He began by stating, "We know that thou art a teacher come from God" (v. 2), probably thinking that Jesus would respond and clarify who he was. But instead, Jesus answered with what seemed like a completely unrelated statement in verse three.

Jesus answered in this way to show him something. Nicodemus' status in the Jewish community and his knowledge of Scripture were not enough to save him. His birth as a Jew was not enough; he had to be born again spiritually to be a child of God.

To trust in your actions or reputation for your salvation is like moving to a different country and thinking that if you can just look and act like all the citizens of that country you will automatically become a citizen. But this is not how the kingdom of heaven works. No matter who you are or what outwardly good things you have done, you must still be born again—born "from above"—to have a rightful place in God's kingdom. Your heart must be sanctified, or transformed, by the Holy Spirit.

ASK YOURSELF...

In what ways are you tempted to trust in your own ability to look like a Christian instead of the transformative work of the Spirit in your heart?

PRAYING TO YOUR HEAVENLY FATHER

- *Praise* God for the change he has worked in your heart.
- *Confess* your own hypocrisy.
- *Thank* God for making you a citizen of the kingdom of heaven.

JOHN 3:7-8

Marvel not that I said unto thee, Ye must be born again.

The wind bloweth where it listeth, and thou hearest the sound thereof, but canst not tell whence it cometh, and whither it goeth: **so is every one that is born of the Spirit.**

DAY 15 – **LIKE THE WIND**

What exactly is this rebirth of the Spirit about which Jesus spoke here? Today we often refer to it as regeneration. Regeneration occurs when the Holy Spirit puts the new life of Christ in the heart of someone who is dead in sin, making them spiritually alive as a child of God. We do not know exactly when regeneration happens. We cannot physically see regeneration take place as you could witness the birth of a new baby. But we can see the effect of it on the believer.

To help Nicodemus (and us) understand this spiritual reality, Jesus used the picture of wind. No one has ever seen the wind. But when we hear the leaves rustling in the trees, see the branches waving back and forth, or pick up debris after a powerful storm, we see evidence of what the wind has done. Like the wind, the Holy Spirit is invisible, yet its work is powerful and life changing. The wind cannot be controlled by human beings, and neither can the Spirit.

Today we have an even better understanding of the wind than they did in Nicodemus' day. Advances in modern meteorology have given scientists a much better idea of how the weather works. Yet even the most advanced computer models cannot exactly predict what the wind will do. The exact movements of the wind and the Holy Spirit are both unknown to us but operate according to God's sovereign and perfect plan.

One of God's attributes is that he is incomprehensible, meaning that he is beyond human understanding. Our limited human minds will never be able to fully understand all that God is and all that he does. Yet God reveals everything that we need to know to believe. Jesus assured Nicodemus here that he did not need to fully understand how regeneration happens in order to believe that it does happen. And by faith, we too can believe in things that we have not seen (Heb. 11:1).

DAY 15 – LIKE THE WIND

ASK YOURSELF...

How do you see evidence of the work of the Holy Spirit in your own heart and life?

....
....
....
....

PRAYING TO YOUR HEAVENLY FATHER

- Pray the words of Psalm 145:3, "Great is the Lord and greatly to be *praised*; and his greatness is unsearchable."
- *Thank* God for the work of regeneration that he has done in your heart.
- *Ask* the Lord to work faith in your heart to believe even when you do not fully understand how he works.

....
....
....
....
....
....
....
....
....
....

JOHN 3:9-13

Nicodemus answered and said unto him, How can these things be?

Jesus answered and said unto him, Art thou a master of Israel, and knowest not these things?

Verily, verily, I say unto thee, We speak that we do know, and testify that we have seen; and ye receive not our witness.

If I have told you earthly things, and ye believe not, **how shall ye believe,** if I tell you of heavenly things?

And no man hath ascended up to heaven, but he that came down from heaven, even the Son of man which is in heaven.

DAY 16 – BELIEVING THE BASICS

As Nicodemus continued to talk to Jesus, he remained puzzled by his words and asked in verse 9, "How can these things be?" Jesus gently rebuked Nicodemus by reminding him that he should have already known and understood all of this because not only is it revealed in nature but also in the Old Testament Scriptures (such as Ezekiel 36 and 37).

Jesus also went on to explain why he was able to teach these things "verily, verily" (v. 11), meaning *with certainty*. He was not just a great prophet, but the Son of God. He came directly from heaven (v. 13), giving him authority that no other prophet had.

Regeneration is a basic, foundational part of the Christian faith. If Nicodemus could not understand "earthly things" such as the salvation of God's people on this earth, how could Jesus go on to teach him "heavenly things" such as the glories of eternal life?

It is not clear from this passage whether Nicodemus truly believed. But we read later in John that Nicodemus defended Jesus in front of the Sanhedrin (John 7:50) and prepared Jesus' body for burial with Joseph of Arimathaea (John 19:39). This seems to indicate that he did believe what Jesus taught him. Jesus' words had a powerful effect on him just as they have a powerful effect on believers today.

Do you appreciate the instruction that you receive from your parents, teachers, and pastor in the basic truths of the Christian faith? Are there times that you are tempted to take this instruction for granted because it feels repetitive and boring? The doctrines that you are learning now are the most important thing that you will learn in your life. This knowledge is essential for you to grow and mature in the Christian faith. Continued study of Scripture will equip you to distinguish what is good and what is evil as you must make many difficult choices throughout the rest of your life. But as Hebrews 5:12–14 points out, you need to drink the milk before you can dig into the meat of God's word.

ASK YOURSELF...

Do you understand and believe all of the major truths of the Christian faith?

....
....
....
....

Is there anything that you have heard recently in a sermon or lesson that you did not understand? Write down your questions to ask a parent or your pastor.

....
....
....
....

PRAYING TO YOUR HEAVENLY FATHER

- *Thank* the Lord for revealing himself to you through creation and the word so that you may believe.
- *Confess* when you have not given your attention to these things as you should.
- *Ask* God to work a love for his truth in your heart.

....
....
....
....
....
....
....
....
....
....

JOHN 3:14-17

And as Moses lifted up the serpent in the wilderness, even so must the Son of man be lifted up:

That whosoever believeth in him should not perish, but have eternal life.

For **God so loved** the world, that he gave his only begotten Son, that whosoever believeth in him should not perish, but have everlasting life.

For God sent not his Son into the world to condemn the world; but that the world through him might be saved.

DAY 17 – **AMAZING LOVE**

These verses are a beautiful summary of the message of Jesus' ministry. We often refer to it as the "gospel"—the good news of salvation in Jesus. Do you remember from Numbers 21:4–9 that God sent poisonous snakes to punish the people for their sin of murmuring against God? But he also provided a means of deliverance from this punishment. Moses was commanded to hold up a bronze snake on a pole before them. If the people looked up at the bronze snake, their lives would be saved.

The bronze snake was the gracious means that God used to give life-saving healing from the deadly poison of the snakes. In the same way, Jesus being lifted up on the cross is how God saves his people from the death they deserve because of their sin. Nicodemus was being challenged to look in faith to Jesus for two things: healing from sin and eternal life. Soon the Son of God would be lifted up on the cross because of the immense love that God has for his people.

How do you know that your parents love you? Is it because your dad dedicates his life to working hard so that you have a safe place to live and food to eat? Is it that your mom dedicates so much of her own time and energy to taking care of the needs of you and your siblings?

In Jesus' death on the cross we see the most powerful expression of love of all time. Our heavenly Father sacrificed his most precious, "only begotten" Son to save his people from all over the world. And with this loving sacrifice comes the promise of Romans 8:32: "He that spared not his own Son, but delivered him up for us all, how shall he not with him also freely give us all things?"

DAY 17 – AMAZING LOVE

ASK YOURSELF...

How does thinking about God's amazing love affect the way you worship him?

....
....
....
....

How are you called to reflect this love to those around you?

....
....
....
....

PRAYING TO YOUR HEAVENLY FATHER

- *Praise* Jehovah for the unchanging love he has for you.
- *Thank* God for showing his love by sending his only begotten Son to die on the cross.
- *Ask* the Spirit to work in your heart to reflect this love to others.

JOHN 3:18-21

He that believeth on him is not condemned: but he that believeth not is condemned already, because he hath not believed in the name of the only begotten Son of God.

And this is the condemnation, that light is come into the world, and men loved darkness rather than light, because their deeds were evil.

For **every one that doeth evil hateth the light**, neither cometh to the light, lest his deeds should be reproved.

But he that doeth truth cometh to the light, that his deeds may be made manifest, that they are wrought in God.

DAY 18 – **LOVING ADMONITION**

All men are attracted to the darkness. Since the fall, we naturally pursue it and run from the light (Rom. 8:7). Apart from the work of the Spirit no man would ever be drawn to the light. Only God's grace can change our hearts to see our need for it.

As we read in John 1, Jesus came into the world as truth and light. He exposed our sin but also revealed that there is life in the Light for those who believe. John returns to the imagery of light and darkness in today's reading. Do you see the contrast between those who believe the gospel message and those who do not? God's judgment on those who do not believe is that he gives them over to their sin; he allows them to live in the darkness. They face this condemnation already in this life and then even more so for eternity in hell.

People who love the darkness ignore the revelation of God in creation. They refuse to read his word and hear it preached. This makes sense because they don't want to hear that they are walking in sin. They separate themselves from the church and from family and friends—those who try to lovingly show them the error of their ways.

As believers, our sins are exposed by the light too. This light comes to us through the preaching of the word on Sunday and through our personal study of God's word. It also comes from the words of our fellow believers or even through admonitions from church leaders.

We should be thankful for these admonitions. Yet how often do we truly appreciate our sin being pointed out? In our sinful pride, we are much more likely to respond defensively than to express our gratitude to those exposing our sin. You may also hesitate to point out sin in others because you are afraid of their reaction. But admonishing each other is part of our calling as brothers and sisters in Christ (Prov. 27:17, Rom. 15:14). And it is the responsibility of your church leaders to use Christian discipline to admonish you if you are walking in darkness.

ASK YOURSELF...

Do you dare to lovingly point out sin in the lives of your godly friends?

What is your response when your sin is pointed out by a fellow believer? Humble thanks? Or anger and excuses?

PRAYING TO YOUR HEAVENLY FATHER

- *Ask* for humility to graciously receive admonition from others.
- *Confess* a sin that you are tempted to love more than God and do not want to give up.
- *Thank* the Lord for sending the Light into the world to save his people from eternal darkness.

JOHN 3:22-30

After these things came Jesus and his disciples into the land of Judaea; and there he tarried with them, and baptized.

And John also was baptizing in Aenon near to Salim, because there was much water there: and they came, and were baptized.

For John was not yet cast into prison.

Then there arose a question between some of John's disciples and the Jews about purifying.

And they came unto John, and said unto him, Rabbi, he that was with thee beyond Jordan, to whom thou barest witness, behold, the same baptizeth, and all men come to him.

John answered and said, A man can receive nothing, except it be given him from heaven.

Ye yourselves bear me witness, that I said, I am not the Christ, but that I am sent before him.

He that hath the bride is the bridegroom: but the friend of the bridegroom, which standeth and heareth him, rejoiceth greatly because of the bridegroom's voice: this my joy therefore is fulfilled.

He must increase, but I must decrease.

DAY 19 – **HE MUST INCREASE**

While disputing with some of the Jews, John the Baptist's loyal disciples heard about Jesus' ministry nearby in Judea and the fact that it was drawing large crowds of people. These disciples were very concerned that so many people were following Jesus. They seemed to think that he and John the Baptist were competing to see who could get the most followers.

John's answer when they brought their concerns to him made clear that this was not the case. First, he pointed out that his ministry was a gift from God (v. 27). Then he reminded them again that he was not the Messiah. He was called to prepare the way for Jesus (v. 28). It was God's will that Jesus become greater and John become less.

John the Baptist used the example of a wedding party to illustrate the difference between his ministry and Jesus' ministry. Jesus is the groom, and his people are the bride. John the Baptist is the best man. The job of the best man at a wedding is to support and assist the groom as he is joined to the bride. It would be inappropriate and selfish for the best man to try to put the focus on himself at the wedding instead of the groom. Unlike his disciples, John the Baptist was joyful that Jesus' ministry was flourishing because that meant he had carried out this calling as "friend of the bridegroom" well.

This illustration reminds us that there is no place for envy and covetousness in ministry. Pastors and churches should never be in competition because their calling is to promote God's glory and not their own. They must be focused on spreading the gospel instead of boosting their popularity. We are also reminded that there is no place for jealousy in the church. You may not be resentful when others have been given different spiritual gifts from yours. We are all to serve together using our own unique gifts for the glory of God (Rom. 12:3–8).

DAY 19 – HE MUST INCREASE

ASK YOURSELF...

What gifts have you been given that you can use to serve the body of Christ?

....
....
....
....

Have you ever been tempted to seek your own glory instead of God's glory when serving in the church?

....
....
....
....

PRAYING TO YOUR HEAVENLY FATHER

- *Thank* the Lord for the good gifts that he has given you.
- *Confess* when you have put your own glory above his.
- *Ask* for him to increase and you to decrease (v. 30).

....
....
....
....
....
....
....
....
....
....

JOHN 3:31-36

He that cometh from above is above all: he that is of the earth is earthly, and speaketh of the earth: he that cometh from heaven is above all.

And what he hath seen and heard, that he testifieth; and no man receiveth his testimony.

He that hath received his testimony hath set to his seal that **God is true**.

For he whom God hath sent speaketh the words of God: for God giveth not the Spirit by measure unto him.

The Father loveth the Son, and hath given all things into his hand.

He that believeth on the Son hath everlasting life: and he that believeth not the Son shall not see life; but the wrath of God abideth on him.

DAY 20 – **GOD IS TRUE**

Jesus was greater than all the prophets that came before him, including John the Baptist. As one who came from heaven, he was a firsthand witness to the things of God. All the previous prophets only knew God through revelation, but Jesus had a personal, loving relationship with his Father. The Old Testament prophets had been given a measure of the Spirit, but as the Son of God Jesus had the fullness of it. His words are the words of God.

The proof of Jesus' deity and authority is undeniable. Yet as John the Baptist pointed out, only a few people out of the crowds believed and all others rejected Jesus' teaching. To reject the message that Jesus brought from heaven is to call God a liar. The apostle John wrote in 1 John 5:10, "He that believeth on the Son of God hath the witness in himself: he that believeth not God hath made him a liar; because he believeth not the record that God gave of his Son."

The penalty for this unbelief is serious. Those who reject the testimony of Jesus experience the wrath of God, not just once, but forever. Verse 36 says that the wrath of God "abideth," meaning it is continually present on them. This verse also states that those who do not believe in Jesus will not have eternal life in heaven and they will not experience any foretaste of this blessed life on the earth either. Believing the truth about Jesus is a matter of life and death!

These serious consequences also come on those today who do not believe in the Son of God as he is revealed in Scripture. This unbelief can be an outright denial or even something more subtle such as debating certain parts of God's word, doubting aspects of God's character, or a lack of trust in the promises that he has made in Christ. Any denial of the truth of Scripture is to call God a liar.

ASK YOURSELF...

Is there any part of Scripture that you have questions about or are tempted to doubt? Write down these questions and doubts to discuss with a parent, elder, or pastor.

PRAYING TO YOUR HEAVENLY FATHER

- *Praise* the Lord for his truth and justice.
- *Thank* your heavenly Father for revealing the truth to you in his infallible word.
- *Ask* the petition of Mark 9:24, "Lord, I believe; help thou mine unbelief!"

JOHN 4:1-9

When therefore the Lord knew how the Pharisees had heard that Jesus made and baptized more disciples than John,

(Though Jesus himself baptized not, but his disciples,)

He left Judaea, and departed again into Galilee.

And he must needs go through Samaria.

Then cometh he to a city of Samaria, which is called Sychar, near to the parcel of ground that Jacob gave to his son Joseph.

Now Jacob's well was there. Jesus therefore, being wearied with his journey, sat thus on the well: and it was about the sixth hour.

There cometh a woman of Samaria to draw water: Jesus saith unto her, Give me to drink.

(For his disciples were gone away unto the city to buy meat.)

Then saith the woman of Samaria unto him, How is it that thou, being a Jew, askest drink of me, which am a woman of Samaria? for **the Jews have no dealings with the Samaritans.**

DAY 21 – **LOVE WITHOUT PREJUDICE**

When the Assyrians conquered Israel in 722 BC, they exiled most of the people. They left behind only the poorest and lowliest people who they thought were not worthy of being taken captive. Those who were left behind eventually intermarried with non-Jewish people from the surrounding areas and their offspring became the people known as the Samaritans.

The Samaritans and the Jews who eventually returned from captivity did not get along. Although they had common ancestry, most Jews were prejudiced against the Samaritans and avoided contact with them as much as possible. The hostility between the two groups even led to open fighting at times. But as Jesus made the journey from Judea to Galilee, he chose to go directly through Samaria instead of going around as many Jews would have chosen to do.

While in Samaria, he stopped to rest at Jacob's well in Sychar and commanded a woman to draw him some water to drink. A devout Jew would have been astounded by Jesus' choice to go through Samaria, and they would have been even more appalled that he would dare speak to a woman of Samaria. Jesus's own disciples were shocked to see him speak with her.

This was not just any Samaritan woman. The fact that she was coming to draw water alone in the middle of the day instead of coming in the morning or evening with all the other women showed that she was a social outcast. She herself was amazed that Jesus would ask her for a drink of water. Since the Jews thought the Samaritans were unclean, most would never have shared a water jug with her.

But Jesus had no use for social norms or prejudice in his ministry. He talked to people from all walks of life, whether they were Jewish leaders or immoral Samaritan women. Race or social status did not put anyone beneath Jesus' notice, and these factors should not cause anyone to be beneath your notice either.

DAY 21 – LOVE WITHOUT PREJUDICE

ASK YOURSELF...

What are some of your own personal prejudices?

....
....
....
....

Have you ever let these biases get in the way of befriending someone or sharing the gospel with them?

....
....
....
....

PRAYING TO YOUR HEAVENLY FATHER

- *Praise* the Lord for his goodness in saving people from all different nations and walks of life.
- *Thank* your heavenly Father for the beautiful diversity of the church.
- *Ask* for the help of his Spirit to keep you from the sin of partiality (James 2:1–13).

....
....
....
....
....
....
....
....
....
....

JOHN 4:10-15

Jesus answered and said unto her, If thou knewest the gift of God, and who it is that saith to thee, Give me to drink; thou wouldest have asked of him, and he would have given thee living water.

The woman saith unto him, Sir, thou hast nothing to draw with, and the well is deep: from whence then hast thou that living water?

Art thou greater than our father Jacob, which gave us the well, and drank thereof himself, and his children, and his cattle?

Jesus answered and said unto her, Whosoever drinketh of this water shall thirst again:

But **whosoever drinketh of the water that I shall give him shall never thirst**; but the water that I shall give him shall be in him a well of water springing up into everlasting life.

The woman saith unto him, Sir, give me this water, that I thirst not, neither come hither to draw.

DAY 22 – **THE LIVING WATER**

As Jesus continued to speak to this woman of Samaria, he told her that if she knew who he really was she would ask him to give her a drink and he would give her living water. Like Nicodemus, the woman takes Jesus literally and does not understand him. "Art thou greater than our father Jacob?" she asks. Jacob dug this well and his ancestors had been getting water from it for 2,000 years. The woman did not realize that Jesus was using water here as an earthly illustration of the Holy Spirit and thirst to signify a search for satisfaction and peace.

If this Samaritan woman was to simply drink water from Jacob's well, her thirst would be quenched for a little while. But each day she would have to come back again to draw more water. With his divine knowledge, Jesus knew that she was looking for spiritual satisfaction in a similar way. She had tried to find happiness by marrying many different men and living an immoral life, yet as each relationship ended, she was still left lonely and wanting more.

How do you try to quench your spiritual thirst with earthly water? Do you try to satisfy your physical desires by giving in to hours of distraction on your phone or playing video games? Or the pleasure of ungodly relationships? Or the high of drugs or alcohol? These things may feel good in the moment, but anything apart from Jesus will always leave you wanting more. None of these physical things can offer more than temporary satisfaction.

You need the living water that Jesus is speaking of here—the "well of water springing up into everlasting life" (v. 14). It is only by being united with Christ through the Spirit that you can have true peace in this life and true happiness for eternity. In heaven there will be no more thirst and Jesus will lead his people to the "living fountains of waters" (Rev. 7:15–17).

ASK YOURSELF…

Where are you tempted to find satisfaction apart from Jesus?

How does it leave you wanting more in the end?

PRAYING TO YOUR HEAVENLY FATHER

- *Thank* God for the gift of his Spirit in your heart.
- *Confess* your sin of searching for satisfaction in lesser earthly things instead of in Christ.
- *Ask* the Lord to work his peace, which exceeds human understanding, in your heart and mind through Christ (Phil. 4:7).

JOHN 4:16-19

Jesus saith unto her, Go, call thy husband, and come hither.

The woman answered and said, I have no husband. Jesus said unto her, Thou hast well said, I have no husband:

For thou hast had five husbands; and he whom thou now hast is not thy husband: in that saidst thou truly.

The woman saith unto him, Sir, I perceive that thou art a prophet.

DAY 23 – **A SAVIOR OF SINNERS**

The Samaritan woman with whom Jesus sat and talked personally was a known adulteress. She had been married multiple times and was living in adultery. How was it that the Son of God would sit and talk to such a wicked woman? Shouldn't he have kept his distance as any pious Jew (and probably even his own disciples) would have done?

Instead, Jesus approached her with love and encouragement. He gently pricked the woman's conscience by asking her about her husband. He called out her sin to show her why she needed the living water that they were just talking about. And he showed her who he was by revealing his divine knowledge of her sin even when she tried to cover it up.

Jesus' countercultural behavior makes perfect sense when we remember why he came to the earth. In Mark 2:17 when the scribes and Pharisees questioned why Jesus ate with publicans and sinners, he replied, "They that are whole have no need of the physician, but they that are sick: I came not to call the righteous, but sinners to repentance." This woman was one of God's children—the sinners that Jesus came to save.

Paul wrote in 1 Timothy 1:15, "Christ Jesus came into the world to save sinners; of whom I am chief." Your heavenly Father already knows about all your sins just as he knew the sins of the woman at the well. There is no sin that you have committed in the past that is too bad or too shameful for him to forgive. There is no sin to which you are currently enslaved from which he cannot save you.

The devil likes to whisper in our ears that we have gone too far this time and that God can never forgive us for what we have done. This is a lie! God's power has no limits. By the power of his Spirit, you can confess and repent of even your most shameful sins and turn from them (Acts 2:38).

DAY 23 – A SAVIOR OF SINNERS

ASK YOURSELF...

Do you have a sin that you have not confessed to God because you do not think he will forgive you? Bring it to him in prayer.

....
....
....
....

If you are truly sorry for this sin but you continue to struggle with it, ask a parent or friend to keep you accountable.

....
....
....
....

PRAYING TO YOUR HEAVENLY FATHER

- *Praise* the Lord for the mercy and grace that he shows to you, an undeserving sinner.
- *Confess* the words of Psalm 51, David's prayer of repentance after his sin with Bathsheba.
- *Ask* for the strength to fight against your sin by the power of the Holy Spirit.

....
....
....
....
....
....
....
....
....
....

JOHN 4:20-24

Our fathers worshipped in this mountain; and ye say, that in Jerusalem is the place where men ought to worship.

Jesus saith unto her, Woman, believe me, the hour cometh, when ye shall neither in this mountain, nor yet at Jerusalem, worship the Father.

Ye worship ye know not what: we know what we worship: for salvation is of the Jews.

But the hour cometh, and now is, when the true worshippers shall worship the Father in spirit and in truth: for the Father seeketh such to worship him.

God is a Spirit: and **they that worship him must worship him in spirit and in truth.**

DAY 24 – **WORSHIP IN SPIRIT AND TRUTH**

It was clear to this woman that Jesus had great knowledge from heaven. Perhaps, she thought, he would have the answer to an often-debated question between the Jews and the Samaritans. Where is the proper place for worship—Jerusalem or Samaria?

The Jews were God's chosen people in the Old Testament. They had a more complete knowledge of salvation than the Samaritans. Since the Samaritans only held to the first five books of the Old Testament, they did not have a full understanding of God. This lack of understanding, along with the conflict between the two groups created controversy about where they should worship.

In answering her question, Jesus explained how the worship of all believers would change in the New Testament. Just like the worship at the temple in Jerusalem, worship on Mt. Gerizim would not last forever. But Jesus also looked forward to the near future when true worship would be distinguished from false worship, not by the location where someone worships, but by whether they worship in spirit and in truth.

In the New Testament, believers can be from any nation and worship God anywhere because they have his Spirit in them. Our bodies are temples of the Holy Spirit (1 Cor. 6:19). But we must also worship him in truth. This means that we must worship as God has commanded us to do so in his word instead of following our own desires. The knowledge of God is vital for proper worship of him. Yet true worship is not just about going through the right motions and saying the right things. It comes from the heart.

The worship of believers will change yet again in heaven. How amazing it will be to worship without any separation between you and your heavenly Father! Do you look forward to eternity when you will be able to worship in the actual presence of the living God (Rev. 21:22)?

ASK YOURSELF…

How is Jesus' instruction to worship in Spirit and in truth so different from the feelings-based worship that is so popular today?

How can you worship God from the heart instead of just going through the motions?

PRAYING TO YOUR HEAVENLY FATHER

- *Thank* God for the gift of his Spirit that enables you to worship him today.
- *Ask* God to work in your heart and mind so that you worship him in spirit and in truth.
- *Praise* God with Mary's words from Luke 1:46–47, "My soul doth magnify the Lord, and my spirit hath rejoiced in God my Saviour."

JOHN 4:25-30

The woman saith unto him, I know that Messias cometh, which is called Christ: when he is come, he will tell us all things.

Jesus saith unto her, I that speak unto thee am he.

And upon this came his disciples, and marvelled that he talked with the woman: yet no man said, What seekest thou? or, Why talkest thou with her?

The woman then left her waterpot, and went her way into the city, and saith to the men,

Come, see a man, which told me all things that ever I did: is not this the Christ?

Then they went out of the city, and came unto him.

DAY 25 – **A PASSION FOR CHRIST**

The Samaritan woman must not have been completely satisfied with Jesus' answer about worship because she responded that when the Messiah comes, he will explain the truth. Then Jesus revealed to her, "I that speak unto thee am he" (v. 26). The woman was overcome with joy and excitement that she had met the Messiah. She left her water jug behind, no longer concerned with her need for water.

Then she eagerly went into the town, public embarrassment and shame forgotten, to tell all of the people she had previously been avoiding about Jesus. She had no qualifications to witness to them except the fact that she had met the Messiah. But still they believed her and came to see him for themselves.

Did you ever start a new hobby or meet someone that you really like and find that you just can't stop talking about them? We cannot help talking about the things that excite us. Whatever is consuming our thoughts will influence our conversations.

Do you have the same excitement to tell others about Jesus? Or do you find yourself not really speaking about him to others at all? It is easy to get complacent in sharing your love of Jesus with others when you are distracted by the business of day-to-day life. Could it be that you are not spending enough time beholding the glory of God in Scripture because you are too preoccupied with school, work, relationships, and hobbies?

As you go through the book of John, take the opportunity to marvel at the glory of your Savior. Remember how exciting and life-changing the truth of the gospel is even if you have been hearing it since you were very young. How could you share with others what you are reading? Could you discuss what you are learning with your family and friends, or maybe even with an unbelieving co-worker? Could you post about it on social media?

DAY 25 – A PASSION FOR CHRIST

ASK YOURSELF...

Are you excited to tell others about Jesus?

....
....
....
....

How can you renew your passion for the truth of the gospel?

....
....
....
....

PRAYING TO YOUR HEAVENLY FATHER

- *Thank* God for the revelation of himself that he has given you through his word.
- *Confess* when you have let all your daily life take priority over spending time in God's word.
- *Ask* the Lord for renewed passion to share the good news of who Jesus is with those around you.

....
....
....
....
....
....
....
....
....

JOHN 4:31-38

In the mean while his disciples prayed him, saying, Master, eat.

But he said unto them, I have meat to eat that ye know not of.

Therefore said the disciples one to another, Hath any man brought him ought to eat?

Jesus saith unto them, **My meat is to do the will of him that sent me,** and to finish his work.

Say not ye, There are yet four months, and then cometh harvest? behold, I say unto you, Lift up your eyes, and look on the fields; for they are white already to harvest.

And he that reapeth receiveth wages, and gathereth fruit unto life eternal: that both he that soweth and he that reapeth may rejoice together.

And herein is that saying true, One soweth, and another reapeth.

I sent you to reap that whereon ye bestowed no labour: other men laboured, and ye are entered into their labours.

DAY 26 – TRUE SATISFACTION

When the disciples returned from buying food, they noticed that Jesus had been so busy talking to the Samaritans that he had not eaten yet. They were understandably concerned about him and urged him to eat. But Jesus turned his earthly hunger into a heavenly lesson. He used this opportunity to teach them about the purpose of his short time on this earth and to encourage them in their calling as disciples of Jesus.

As humans we eat to nourish our earthly bodies so that we can go about our day. But we also eat to feel full and satisfied. Hunger is not just an empty feeling that tells us we need to eat. It is an intense craving for what will meet this need. This is why when someone has a strong desire for something other than food, such as winning a game or reaching a goal, people often refer to them as being "hungry" for it.

Do you have a strong desire for something that you think will bring you satisfaction? Do you think that if God would just follow the plan that you have for your life on this earth, then you will be truly happy? Jesus teaches here that true satisfaction is not found in your own earthly desires being fulfilled. The source of his strength and satisfaction was not bread or meat but following the will of his heavenly Father by gathering God's elect people from all nations.

You may think that you know what is best for your life, but the God of infinite knowledge and perfect love knows what is better. You will find true contentment and satisfaction only in carrying out the calling that God has for you on this earth, even if it is very different from what you planned or expected. The profits of earthly work are only temporary, but doing God's work reaps eternal benefits.

ASK YOURSELF...

When you are making decisions about your future, do you seek God's will or just your own will?

....
....
....
....

How can you seek God's will for your life?

....
....
....
....

PRAYING TO YOUR HEAVENLY FATHER

- *Praise* the Lord for his sovereignty.
- *Confess* how you may be frustrated with the way God is directing your life.
- *Ask* for grace to submit your desires to God's will and look to his word to guide your decisions.

....
....
....
....
....
....
....
....
....
....

JOHN 4:39-45

And many of the Samaritans of that city believed on him for the saying of the woman, which testified, He told me all that ever I did.

So when the Samaritans were come unto him, they besought him that he would tarry with them: and he abode there two days.

And many more believed because of his own word;

And said unto the woman, Now we believe, not because of thy saying: for we have heard him ourselves, and know that this is indeed the Christ, the Saviour of the world.

Now after two days he departed thence, and went into Galilee.

For Jesus himself testified, that **a prophet hath no honour in his own country**.

Then when he was come into Galilee, the Galilaeans received him, having seen all the things that he did at Jerusalem at the feast: for they also went unto the feast.

DAY 27 – **A PROPHET WITHOUT HONOR**

Jesus spent two more days teaching the Samaritans before continuing north to Galilee. It is worthwhile to note the contrast between the two groups described in this passage—the Samaritans, who were Gentiles, and the Galileans, who were Jews. How did each group receive Jesus' teaching?

Many of the Samaritans believed in Jesus at first because of the amazing things that the woman at the well had told them about him. But as they continued to listen to his teaching, their belief was confirmed. They truly received him as the promised Christ, confessing him to be "the Saviour of the world" (v. 42).

When Jesus went on to Galilee, the Jews there welcomed him because of the great signs and wonders that they had seen him work during the festival in Jerusalem. They were fascinated by what he could do, yet they did not truly believe and give him the honor that he deserved as the Messiah.

Although Jesus had been born in Bethlehem in Judea, Nazareth in Galilee was the place where he grew up. Therefore, Nazareth is often referred to as his hometown. This is what verse 44 means when it calls Galilee "his own country." The people of Jesus' homeland were interested only in his miracles and politics. As a nation they would ultimately reject Jesus as their Savior.

Many people today have the same attitude as the Galileans when they decide to come to church. They come because they are attracted to the idea of Jesus, and they want to see what he can do for them. They are simply looking for a quick fix to all their problems. They fail to see that their primary need is salvation from sin, not from their circumstances. They are not willing to repent of their sins and fully submit to Jesus' authority for their life.

DAY 27 – A PROPHET WITHOUT HONOR

ASK YOURSELF...

Are you ever tempted to have a "quick fix" attitude when coming to church or reading the Bible?

Why is it so important to remember that God's word is primarily about him, not about you?

PRAYING TO YOUR HEAVENLY FATHER

- *Thank* the Lord for redeeming his people from all over the world.
- *Confess* an area of your life where you are not fully submitting to God's authority.
- *Ask* for the grace to give God the honor he deserves.

JOHN 4:46-54

So Jesus came again into Cana of Galilee, where he made the water wine. And there was a certain nobleman, whose son was sick at Capernaum.

When he heard that Jesus was come out of Judaea into Galilee, he went unto him, and besought him that he would come down, and heal his son: for he was at the point of death.

Then said Jesus unto him, Except ye see signs and wonders, ye will not believe.

The nobleman saith unto him, Sir, come down ere my child die.

Jesus saith unto him, **Go thy way; thy son liveth**. And the man believed the word that Jesus had spoken unto him, and he went his way.

And as he was now going down, his servants met him, and told him, saying, Thy son liveth.

Then enquired he of them the hour when he began to amend. And they said unto him, Yesterday at the seventh hour the fever left him.

DAY 27 – A PROPHET WITHOUT HONOR

So the father knew that it was at the same hour, in the which Jesus said unto him, Thy son liveth: and himself believed, and his whole house.

This is again the second miracle that Jesus did, when he was come out of Judaea into Galilee.

DAY 28 – **WORDS OF LIFE**

The nobleman who came to Jesus in Cana appeared at first to have the same attitude as his fellow Galileans that you read about yesterday. He heard about Jesus' great miracles and came to him with his own problem. This nobleman had a son who was sick, near to death, and he desperately wanted Jesus to come and heal him.

Jesus began by rebuking the nobleman in order to test his faith, but the nobleman persisted. He pleaded again for Jesus to come and heal his son, having no other options. Jesus then granted his request and told the nobleman that his son was healed, and he should go his way.

The fact that the man believed Jesus shows that he had great faith. First, Cana and Capernaum were sixteen miles apart. And second, he did not actually find out that his son was healed until he arrived home the next day. Yet the man took Jesus at his word and went on his way. We read that not only did he believe, but also his entire household.

This is the second major sign (of seven) that John records in his gospel account. It serves as yet another proof of Jesus' deity. Only one who was truly God could perform a miracle like this. This sign also put on display the authority that Jesus has over life and death. The healing of the nobleman's son is a picture of what Jesus does for each and every one of his people. His words bring both life and salvation.

By nature, you were dead in sin with no hope for recovery (Eph. 2:1). But God in his great mercy came to you in your desperate need with life-giving power. He worked true faith in your heart so that you have knowledge of your sin and confidence in your Savior—the one who took your sickness and misery upon himself and suffered in your place so that you could be healed (Isa. 53:4, 1 Pet. 2:24).

DAY 28 – WORDS OF LIFE

ASK YOURSELF...

Why is it important for all believers, even mature ones, to be reminded of their sin and great need for a Savior?

What means has God given you to do this?

PRAYING TO YOUR HEAVENLY FATHER

- *Confess* your sin and need for a Savior.
- *Praise* the Lord for his great mercy.
- *Thank* God for working new life in your heart.